The No No Zone

Camryn + Caden
May God Bless
+ Protect you!

Keli

KELI MATTHEWS

THE NoNo ZONE
Written by KELI MATTHEWS
Edited by ESHAM ABDUL GILES
Illustration & Cover Design by
Orlando Feliz
For further information about this book, write all inquires
and permissions to;
Focus Write Inspire LLC.
PO BOX 373
NEWARK, NJ 07101
www.FocusWriteInspire.com
Library of Congress Cataloging-in-Publication Data is
available.
Library of Congress Control Number: 2014959457
ISBN-13: 9780692352991

esham abdul giles

FOCUS WRITE INSPIRE PUBLISHING

DEDICATION

This book is dedicated to my children and grandchildren.

You are all the wind beneath my wings.

May you always be covered and protected by God's grace.

Love,

Mima

Parental advisory: This book is to enlighten our children about inappropriate touching. It will teach our children the proper names for their private parts and importance of reporting sexual abuse. My children and I pray that this book will assist in the prevention of this horrific crime.

It was a beautiful day at The Edna Vaughan Elementary School.

1

2

Ms. Lamb's kindergarten class was excited about going to play on the new playground for recess.

"Everybody get in line quietly", said Mrs. Lamb.

Down the hall and out the door the class went. "No running, pushing, or shoving" said Ms. Lamb.

3

4

Kajae' and Susie wanted to try the sliding board first.   Kiree and Ernesto decided to swing from the monkey bars.

5

Susie ran up the ladder, slid down the slide, and landed in the dirt on her buttocks.

7

8

Kajae' hurried over, "are you okay?"

"No, Susie replied crying! "I hurt my buttocks, can you check it for me?"

9

10

"NO!" SHOUTED KAJAE'. "THAT'S A PRIVATE PART IN YOUR NONO ZONE."

11

12

"What's a NoNo Zone" said Susie? "Your mommy and daddy never told you about your NoNo Zone" asked Kajae'?
"No," said Susie.

13

14

Kajae' helped Susie up and they went to talk under the big maple tree.

15

16

"Girls and boys have three very private body parts. Girls and boys have different parts, but they're all private." Girls have breasts, a vagina, and buttocks.

Boys have a penis, testicles, and buttocks.

These parts are called our NoNo Zone. No one should ever touch you in these places and you should never touch theirs either."

17

Susie asked Kajae'," what should you do if someone does touch you?"

19

"You should always tell someone. You can tell your mommy, your daddy, a teacher, your doctor, a friend, anybody."

21

22

"People who touch you there are BAD." "They sometimes try to trick you or scare you by telling you things like, it's our little secret, or you will get into trouble if you tell, or that they will hurt you or someone you love. Don't ever believe them, that's not true." "You must always tell someone, even if you're scared, TELL!"

24

"Every night before my brother and I go to sleep, we say this prayer and you should too."

26

"Now I lay me down to sleep,

My NoNo Zone for GOD to keep,

But if someone should touch me there,

I will tell, and not be scared."

Amen.

28

Keli Matthews

THE END

ACKNOWLEDGMENTS

To my Lord and Savior Jesus Christ, I thank you for your grace and mercy. I'm humbled by your love for me.

To my mother, thank you for all you sacrificed, your continued prayers, love, support, and encouragement. You mean the world to me.

To my children Ashley, Kyron, Kajae', & Kiree you all are the reason this book even exists. Thank you all for your input, support, and courage.

To my grand babies, Kaiden and Jordyn, you two are the wind beneath my wings. Mema loves you to the moon and back.

To my sisters, Hollee and Kenya, you two are my rocks. You've stood with me and pushed me when I got weary and started to doubt myself. I love you both so much. Thank you for always having my back and never letting me down.

To Pastors Luther and Tanya Johnson and the Incense Prayer and Deliverance family. Your ministry has been such a blessing to me and my children. It was at a service at your church, that I received the instruction to write this book. I am forever thankful for you two.

To Pastor Ernest Vaughan and the New Life Deliverance family. Thank you all for your support, prayers and encouragement. I love you all.

To DeLisa Burns, thank you so much for all your support in my time of need. You were God sent and a blessing. I love you.

To my aunts and uncles, Rosetta, Sharon, Wanda, Lisa, Carla, Ernie, & Gerald thank you all for your support and prayers.

To my best friends, Colette Carter, Cheray Jackson, and Bernadine Banks thank you all for the laughs, talks, tears, prayers, and encouragement. I don't know where I would be without you three.

Keli Matthews

To Susan Sprague-Lee, words cannot express the way I feel about you. You will FOREVER be an angel to me and my children. Your dedication, guidance, and GODLY love for us is amazing. You ROCK!!!!

To my grandparents Ernest & the late Rev. Edna Vaughan, thank you for a solid foundation and for all you both instilled in me. What a great example of GOD's love.

To the late Arvetta Massey Farmer, Aunt Vett you will never know how much you meant to me and my children. Thank you for ALWAYS being there for me when I needed you. You encouraged me daily with that infectious smile and heartfelt laugh. I love and miss you so.

To Pastor Jamal H. Bryant and the Empowerment Temple family, your cyber sanctuary was such a blessing to me in writing this book. I thank GOD for using you to guide me.

To Esham Abdul Giles and the Focus Write Inspire family, thank you for believing in my vision and pushing me every step of the way. I love you E, Edna and Lois are smiling down on us.

To Orlando, thank you for bringing my story to life with your illustrations. Your patience and professionalism is greatly appreciated.

Last but not least, thank you Christopher Jones for your love and support through this process. I love and appreciate you so much. You are definitely "A GIFT FROM GOD!!"

Made in the USA
Columbia, SC
28 April 2020